OTHER PROHIBITED ITEMS

OTHER PROHIBITED ITEMS

Martha Greenwald

THE MISSISSIPPI REVIEW POETRY SERIES
HATTIESBURG 2010

Published by the *Mississippi Review*, Hattiesburg, MS 39406

Manufactured in the United States of America

10 9 8 7 6 5 4 3 2 1

ISBN 978-0-9842652-0-6

ISSN 0047-7559

Mississippi Review Volume 37 Number 3 ~ Book 1 of 3

Poems in this manuscript were previously published in the following magazines, sometimes in slightly altered form: *Best New Poets 2008*, "Other Prohibited Items"; *Cave Wall*, "The Lucille Ball Rose"; *Dogwood*, "FindAnyone.com"; *Grand Street*, "Pensione Cristallo"; *Grolier Poetry Prize Annual*, "Listening to the Car Radio at Night"; *MARGIE*, "Mammatocumulus"; *The Midwest Quarterly*, "Memorandum, re: Garlic Salt," "The Greek Week Tornado," "For Sale by Owner"; *The Notre Dame Review*, "Turbulence, the Truck Driver, and the Waitress"; *Open 24Hours*, "Severe Thunderstorm Warning," "Quarterly Meeting: Late Arrival in a Southern City"; *Poetry*, "1813," "Sunday Afternoon Palindrome," "Edward Hopper Watching *The Petrified Forest*, 1936," "The Story of the Day"; *Press*, "JoAnne from Travel Accounting"; *Shenandoah*, "Addendum"; *Slate*, "The Last Secretary," "September 26, 2001," "Mother's Maiden Name"; *Sycamore Review*, "Generic Princess Book"; *The Threepenny Review*, "At the Checkout."

Mississippi Review is published twice a year by the Center for Writers, The University of Southern Mississippi (AA/EOE/ADAI), 118 College Drive, #5144, Hattiesburg, MS 39406-0001. Editor: Frederick Barthelme. Managing Editor: Rie Fortenberry. Associate Editors: Angela Ball, Steven Barthelme, Julia Johnson. Assistant Editors: Lynn Watson, Elizabeth Wagner, Beth Couture. Subscription rates: $15 per year for individuals, $32 for institutions. Foreign subscriptions $10 per year additional. Single copies $9. *Mississippi Review* wishes to acknowledge the kind support of the National Endowment for the Arts. The views expressed herein are those of the authors, not the editors or sponsors. Printed in the United States of America by McNaughton & Gunn, Inc., P.O. Box 10, Ann Arbor, MI 48176. Distributed in the United States by Ubiquity Distributors, 607 Degraw St., Brooklyn, NY 11217. Archive available through JSTOR. Indexed by *Humanities International Complete*. Special thanks to Dara Wier for selecting the 2010 *Mississippi Review* Poetry Series winners.

CONTENTS

ONE

TWO

THREE

in memory of Martin and Judith Greenwald

and, for Lucy

ONE

Have I conceived all this people? have I begotten them, that thou shouldest say unto me, Carry them in thy bosom, as a nursing father beareth the sucking child, unto the land which thou swarest unto their father?

—Numbers 11:12

CROSSWALK

Black cases swing from their mittens.
Inside—purple velvet, and nestled
in the plush, the dismantled clarinets.

By the time the brothers reach home,
the cases will be furred with snow—
small animals with silver bones
ready for the weekend's hibernation.

OTHER PROHIBITED ITEMS

"... try not to over-think these guidelines."
—Southwest.com Carry-on Tips

No to his bassoon. No to their cricket bat.
No to your robot, her corkscrew, that hatchet.
Good traveler, whose children might be overjoyed—

Next trip, please procure toys that resemble toys.
Policy does not ban pink princess/pirate swords
But for security, we confiscate all backstories

(Though adaptations are few). Item: one wrench
From a beloved uncle's workbench, pilfered
After his funeral, just before the flight. Lost thanks

For his kindnesses, the raucous Christmas pranks—
Although he taught his nephew the lathe, relinquish
The memento at our checkpoint. Item: rose oil,

Decanted by monks, four ounces in a faceted flacon.
Rare, the passenger whispers, hushed, as if pleading
To the lover for whom the secret gift was intended.

Well, her kiss may *be* sublime but no to the perfume's
Ounce of excess; and no to the antique drawknife,
Despite its moonstone handle, studded with marcasite.

Again, mid-shift, a woman about to board a red-eye
Puts her Ziploc on the x-ray conveyor, then flusters
When we screen the bag's contents. The bottles warm

Our gloved hands. Milk rivulets dampen our sleeves.
However, her infant waits at the destination, so toss
Her bottles to the take-bin, foremilk already separating

From hindmilk. No to her umbrella, unruly & floral.
Sorry—storm phobias never justify hollow finials.
No exceptions for the sentimental or exceptional.

Our take-bins swell with keepsakes decades misplaced,
With longings for the heft of a snowglobe balanced
On a small palm. Look inside—old Snow White

Sleeps in a dubious solution. No to her domed sky's
Blizzard. No to the castle, no to apples. Witches lurk
In these woods, and every poisoned pie is gooseberry.

Quarterly Meeting: Late Arrival in a Southern City

—for A.P.G.

The suitcase tows you, an obedient pet;
    creaky-wheeled, old black leatherette
        companion whose innards tangled in the dim

cargo hold somewhere between here & home.
    Faithful, it rallies to shepherd you down
        stark airport corridors, infallible though slow.

Governed by halogens, the Hertz lot is a twilit
    grove of Bradford pears & just-washed white
        sedans. Dispersed blossoms—the sinuses

remember, inflame. Inside, this week's Taurus
    smells of cherry cough drops, french fries, smoke.
        From a dream, one month dead, our mother spoke

while you'd drowsed mid-flight, her lips ulcered,
    sprouting weeds, these same roadside ochre
        stalks whose pollen hovers above the macadam

in eddies. But as a boy, on every December's
    car trip south, wasn't this precisely the juncture
        that woke you—bare oaks to elms, sorrow

recedes in the rear window—pines to green palms,
    their air sulfurous. Father drives, asleep it seems,
        the station wagon set adrift. If you ask mother

for sandwiches, her face glances backward over
    the passenger seat, arms amputated as she reaches
        down to retrieve bread from the red ice chest.

MOTHER'S MAIDEN NAME

Understand the terms, dearest customer:
Before beginning any transaction, we must
Margin your debt with memory. Calculate
3.3% of a snow day, the house sour-sweet,
Vermouth eluding the dark, mildewed ducts.

Upon approval, wander up to their bedroom.
Check the street. Father has veered downhill
To examine a patient's ice-scratched cornea,
His fishtail tracks already filled. For balance
Transfers, open the emerald-lined lingerie

Drawer of her teak bureau—garter buckles,
Hippie beads, packets of envelopes addressed
To her childhood Queens address. Restrictions
May apply but extract the letters, deciphering
The varied crabbed hands of college boyfriends:

Rosenberg Rosenberg what you read is lewd.
From his Bangladesh cubicle, an account rep,
Skewing a New York idiom, makes you spell,
Pronounce, spell, so the name becomes its own
Unknown language. Omit your guarded jokes;

Bad habits and insolvency always fail to amuse.
You are the sole beneficiary to White Shoulders
Rising from the boning of a long-line brassiere.
Please note: at dusk, all grace periods expire;
Thus, winter interest fees will continue to accrue.

AT BRACKNELL

"At last, in his despair, and thinking that the passion
in him would make a miracle, he pulled his shirt away
and tried himself to suckle the child."
> —diary entry of Stopford Brooke as
> reported by Lady Shelley

". . . but what scrutiny can secure the suckling
against the bad effects of her passions . . ."
> —Thomas Trotter, MD 1807

Old rain, milk distilled by nightmare—
Released from her wet nurse, from the sodden
Blue undersides of breasts, Ianthe returned,
Crowned again with stench: Loam, mold,

Goat turds & fennel tea. Worse than disease;
All the nurse's dreams swallowed & souring
In his daughter's body. What visions
Might besiege an infant whose sustenance

Falls from areolas black as eclipse? Crated
Stillborns, a cold winter hearth, soup bones
Rising from a cauldron, geese resurrected,
Feathered ghosts float in muddied broth . . .

But Harriet refused to suckle; corseted,
Primping, she could not even bear to watch
Shelley sing & pace, Ianthe in sickness,
Primrose face nestled & rooted against

Her father's chest. And so he parted his shirt,
Latched her lips to his nipple, a small fevered fish.
If her simple thirst sufficed, she would be fed
From his soul, & once asleep, desire his dreams—

Pamphlets & letters intricately folded, set asail
On the Serpentine. She'd launch two skiffs windward,
Run to the opposite bank, seize the bows leeward
Beneath boundless sky, paper flotilla intact.

Listening to the Car Radio at Night

Tutankhamen's tomb is bare. The blue-jeweled faces
Stolen from their pedestals, as the boy-king's body
Hovered in the bony air. Dick Tracy listens to Dryden Small
Describe the ruined antechamber; two dead guards,
Their skulls shattered by statues, and scrawled on the walls
In blood: *Death to those who enter these rooms.*

Magnifying glass in hand, Tracy cases the burial room
And blurts, *Aha! The man with the violet face!*
Clearly his work, why look at the frieze on this wall,
Dryden, these hieroglyphs are freshly painted. Everybody,
Get your decoder rings! We'll stay here tonight to guard
The sacred sarcophagus—Tracy spreads his coat near a small

Sandstone sphinx and takes a cat nap, while Dryden Small,
Too rattled to close his eyes, roams the musty rooms.
He pockets a scarab amulet, hoping its powers will guard
Them from angry gods, but then, in the torchlight, the gold face
Of the funerary mask groans. Dryden shakes Tracy's body.
Wake up, there's an invisible hand writing on the wall,

Dick, wake up! Dryden reads the message appearing on the wall:
22, 9, 5 . . . static from another city . . . *12, 2,* his voice smaller,
Then incomprehensible. My mother tuned the station, her body
Bridging the front seat to bring me clues from the secret rooms.
That night at the motel, I wouldn't sleep. I lay on a cot facing
The windows, needing to decipher who killed the guards,

Who seized the treasures. In the wind, palm trees guarding
The parking lot sketched pliant shadows on our walls,
Ziggurats floated above my father's sleeping face,
Flaring or sinking when his chest moved. Contained in a small
Pyramid of light, my mother sat between the beds and bathroom.
I could see her traveling silver cocktail set, the black body

Of the case cracked open at her feet, the amber-bodied
Bottle of whiskey on the end table. Safeguarded
In an armchair, she uncoiled her headdress in the room's
Phosphorescent tiers. I studied all undulations on the walls,
To guarantee my parents' breathing. I feared their small
Syncopations of sleep, blank sounds from a face,

The body's abrupt twitching, feet thumping against the wall.
I repeated these gestures, the unseen guardian of a small
Motel room, searching the darkness for a violet face.

THE LUCILLE BALL ROSE

*A striking hybrid tea rose with sweet fragrance and
lavish season-long show of blooms. Distinguished
by glorious color (a perfect match to Lucy's hair).*
—Jackson & Perkins catalogue

Jealous, jealous—the garden envies the television
through the living room's wide bay windows—
decoding the upswept, lacquered hair scarlet
like the credits' opening heart. The maternity top
(emerald, velvet) is a green the garden must match,

stealing chlorophyll from lawns, from trees, until all
is black & grey & white, except the roses, who tell jokes,
to entertain other flowers at night. Petunias get advised
Dress incognito as Tropicana showgirls; the lavender embarks

for Europe on a liner next week. When it rains, pebbles
beat on bongos & the fireflies can concoct elaborate
schemes—unlit, it's easy for them to plot, hide, whisper.
Perfectly disguised, never having known such happiness,
they scribble strategies on the wet screen of soil.

AT THE CHECKOUT

First *Für Elise,* in singsong digital bleeps—
Ignored, the cell's repertoire swells:
Five frenzied bars of Pachelbel, twelve
Seconds of the *Minute Waltz,* beginner's
Exercises for the right hand, begging

To be answered. Your seventh winter.
Practicing chords on the upright, you heard
The phone ring above your sloppy fingerings
Then something like laughter from the kitchen . . .

You hurried to find your mother collapsed
On the linoleum, keening. For an hour no one
Told you her father had died. Four cold months,
When there was no difference between joy and grief,
Summoned from the paisley lining of a stranger's purse.

SEVERE THUNDERSTORM WARNING

Hail falls, our street tympanic. Next door, Chester,
shirtless, lounges on the porch smoothing his milky
parabola of belly. Though his chimes and feeders
flail, my neighbor stays put, one thumb corked

in his navel. So round . . . no, that's how large
I'd have been this week. Beneath an early evening
sitcom, a ribbon of Doppler-predicted subtitles
rewrites the bickering couple's scene—remain

alert, conditions can change spontaneously:
listen for sirens, seek shelter in a low
windowless place. The storm inverts, vast
planes of water slam sideways against shuttered

doors and sills. Chester crosses his ankles, tilts
the chaise farther back. His rain-glazed skin shines.

SEPTEMBER 26, 2001

—Kosair Children's Hospital, 4 AM

Enter the pediatrician in his patriotic scrubs.
Yawning, apologetic, he lifts a blue beribboned
stethoscope to our infant daughter's chest
and listens. Beneath the sheet, her wired feet
swim and dart, toes a school of glowing minnows.

Twice tonight I have half-slept in the recliner
and dreamt of my dead mother at the beach:
Sandy Hook, late summer, the afternoon's sangria
thermos empty, and on the sand beside her
its wake of wine-soaked rinds—at the surf's edge,

a mess of putrid Jersey mussels, and beyond
on the horizon, the South Tower, molten with sunset.
Our daughter has too much heart, so tomorrow
they will ligate the extra arch, tangled round
her trachea like seaweed. Pace the ward,

pace the ward. Store more breast milk in the patient
biohazard freezer. Pause at the nurse's station,
stuffed menagerie pawing four-inch stars-and-stripes.
Hi, Mom! says the resident. Good morning, Dad!
says a nurse. In hospital rhetoric we are everyone's

mother and father, so the parents we pass sleeping
upright in chairs are also our children, and we are theirs.
We all stare toward televisions hung from curtained
partitions like plants—turbaned blossoms,
camouflage leaves, on every screen, the Taliban.

THREE

i. UPS

The humpbacked truck idles at the curb.
Dank with storm, its great brown mouth
belches parcels. And here comes God, dapper
in Bermuda shorts, slipping on the flagstones
as he runs toward the porch. He helps us sign
our name with a stylus, snaps his big book shut.
Then, stacked by the door, four third birthday
boxes . . . the wet cardboard's briny reek wells
tidal up the stairwell, tantrum down the hall—
cereal left to swim all morning in a milky bowl.

ii. The Playhouse

—Five o'clock burlesque of her favorite
preschool friend—the girl who slaps and shrieks,
muddied enunciation, blotchy cheeks. *Be Madison*
daughter demands; understudy for another botched
playdate, thrash as the lilac mesh castle lists East.
O whine, then eat, while your feet, cantilevered
on blocks, turn phantom limbed. Now be a baby,
sleep louder than our neighbor's schnauzer, ape
her teacher (with too-small teeth). Please don't
mime the new boy, a classmate who cannot speak.

iii.   Snow Jar

Stealthy one, those quiet seasons, hidden
between cauliflower, peas and freezer wall—
undone by summer's freak inland hurricane.
Putrid foods trashed, we tip the viscous quart
of amber toward our flashlights and discover
the lost dog-stone she'd mourned last December.
Still, a likeness: gray granite coat, mica-fleck eyes
wide set on a wide head—gone missing that day
she announced *I'll eat wind*, then stood, mouth
agape to the squall, gulping the lake-effect bitters.

GENERIC PRINCESS BOOK

—Family Dollar Store

The homeschooled girls in the toy aisle know
The moon never multiplies in a mermaid's cove.
Almost white, almost beauty, minus snow,

The strip mall's narrow lot is lit with salt.
Today's assignment: arithmetic. Account
For soup bowls & crackers, the plastic geometry

Of laundry baskets. Add 5 clearance dwarves,
The youngest named Deluded, subtract 3 witches,
Less 1 beast who was never truly a beast,

Minus his dungeon, minus his mother who cast
Her only son to this kingdom of eternal endcaps.
(Propped beside old taffy & the aqua towers

Of storage bins, his gladiator torso hides in fur.)
At the wedding feast of his sidekick—an almost
Headless prince—the beast who was never truly

A beast proclaims a decree: his future bride will love
No one, her face fetal, abstracted by moonbeams—
Almost white, almost beauty, minus snow.

Two

But these are all landsmen; of weekdays pent up in lath and plaster—tied to counters, nailed to benches, clinched to desks. How then is this? Are the green fields gone?

—Herman Melville, *Moby Dick*

THE LAST SECRETARY

This morning, in the ladies room mirror,
She realizes her blouse is message-pad pink.

Her whole torso contains choices waiting
To be checked off and dispensed with down the hall . . .

While You Were Out, sickened by the foul air,
What happened? Three calls, four faxes, then

The computer chimes its happy middle C—
New mail. Another and another chain letter:

"Forward this message ten times to find lost loves,
Twenty, and golden fortune will fly into your lap."

Bad luck befalls those who do not participate.
Remember the legendary examples who declined,

Deleted their letters, then died within weeks—
Miss X from Texas, blackened in a fiery wreck;

Janine H, the beautiful, midwestern receptionist,
Drowned on her honeymoon by a mad gondolier.

Who needs uninvited foreboding stapled to the day,
The dread of going home to what was your home,

When instead, by playing along, the power
Of the unsent might retreat at least until noon.

Downstairs, women leave, wrapped in long wool coats.
My dear, what *did* happen while you were out?

Lunch is crackers, a freeze-dried cup of soup.
The peas and carrots bloom in the boiling water.

ADDENDUM

Thirty years old, forty, yet still we daily covet
the covert—mascots and gargoyles propped atop
our monitors, a pastiche of sentries, watch kept

for the boss. If messages to your pal in personnel
resemble minutes or a memo to headquarters
in Milwaukee, no one knows what you're doing,

assuming the work gets done. So exchange
flirty jokes with your green-eyed friend upstairs;
third graders passing notes, the dreary afternoon

saved by chaste communiqué. At 3:45, the day
interminable, marital woes from your brother,
whose address, encoded, wed to numerals,

becomes an electronic esperanto of the past . . .
artg8@clipper, his executive identity a shorthand
for scrawls on spiral notebooks, Minute Men,

bedroom ships launched below the cursor's pulse.
Refill your stained mug with awful coffee, then fire
back analysis of his wife disguised as a chart—

The long commute home remains an hour away . . .
Behind the credenza, the boss skulks. O Camouflage,
our savior, we despise what we do so much.

CANCELLED DRINKS WITH FORMER COLLEAGUE

Because she sat too close beside you at meetings,
drafting cartoons rather than minutes, her overfull
coffee cup splotching your agendas like a muddy

spring storm; because after sneaking a distant lunch
you watched her sigh and crunch fists of antacids
(Clinique Azalea lipstick blurred, an afternoon's

birthmark on her cheek); because candy wrappers
rustling under the desk turned the office autumn
when she pushed off to pirouette in that perfect chair;

because her retriever was reborn as a screensaver,
who fetched and barked all day across the cubicles;
because you'd recognize the syrupy smell of her piss

from any adjacent stall; because you saw her silvered
molars when she yawned, and found them, winking
beneath the fluorescents, perhaps, a little too lovely.

JoAnne, From Travel Accounting

I. Reimbursements

Again it's me, so sorry, calling yet
again about those lost mileage receipts.
Frankly, life has been crazy and I guess
no one should expect any work this week.
Just last night, driving home, I killed a deer.
Oh, I'm alright, or right as this gal *can* be.
Shapes shot out from the road's shoulder.
I had three options: Hit the deer, hit a tree,
or veer straight into an oncoming Exxon truck.
I hit the deer, steered toward it to tell the truth.
Given choices but no time at all to think
—I'd always wondered, sweetie, what I'd do—
Quite the lesson to learn at my age really.
Tired, in the dark, I chose what had chosen me.

II. Minutes

Item: As per the remarks of our Chair,
my transcriptions concern the committee
(i.e., a deceased nominee approved three
defeated policies). I'd show notes to verify
I was befuddled, seated near the IT boys
(how young they smell in overworn sweaters).
My errors: agendas of malted milk, cut weeds,
sweat. And, lately, no matter the weather, 2 PM
showers take our office by surprise. This stuns me
—explain, please, why I always fall for the trick—
though I know the sound is just the newest hire,
a loner who jogs at lunch, returning to her keyboard.
Noted: The absentees remain in the conference room.
Resolved: The Chair's assistant types like the rain.

III. In Triplicate

You forgot to deduct his disallowed
meals, and forwarded one copy, not three.
Eveline, my friend who did disbursements,
hated such mistakes. Maybe you'd met?
She was eleven inches shorter than me,
and her feet, hidden every season in high heels,
belonged on the body of a nine-year-old girl.
Last March, the thin soles iced through to her toes.
She said I was funny—note that no one can claim
fancy snacks or souvenirs—but she was funny too.
All my life, often and always, I have been called
ambiguous. She's passed. I'd be frank, if asked.
More than once, I crouched beside our desks
and warmed Eveline's small feet in my hands.

FIND ANYONE.COM

But there are those we should not try to find,
like you, affable high-school friend, ferreted

out by your chem class partner twenty years
after her tincture imploded on the black

slate desk. The only injury an asterisk of flesh
under her right wrist. Still she messages, calls,

bloating the incident, inventing details;
she remembers you popular, pretty.

Where is the oddball girl, the self-pity
cloaking you like a gray wool coat?

The less she recalls the more you doubt
your own relics, half-friends evoked

by stoplight glances, long lines at the bank . . .
the teller's forearms, her plump neck—

Experiment: for a password & thirty bucks
why not funnel the past into a beaker, locate

the temp you worked beside that January
morning the Challenger blew up? Her anguish,

vaporized, filled the volume of the office,
displacing even the air in your desk drawers.

So, post-pleasantries, if she recognizes your
name, would you reconstitute that sadness,

confess how upon hearing of any catastrophe
you still think of her, public despair distilled

to the memory of one woman wrecked in a cubicle?
Days later, you found her alone in the copy room—

Revise your lab. Report, instead, this outcome:
Tap dancing between cartons, synchronized

to the collator's jumbled staccato, she seized
your hands & spun, making you the center

of her compass. Then the machine stopped,
pages stacked—last week's minutes haloed

by doodled astronauts, spacesuits beginning
ascent, buoyant in the margins of the documents.

MEMORANDUM RE: GARLIC SALT

Tone's Inc. Headquarters

This is to inform you that it was snowing;
    as our city saw, a storm that did not end for weeks.
        This was not the beginning of things.
        It has been a winter of frail women
        slipping on the way to the mailbox
        and never knowing warmth again.

In our warehouse there was a problem:
    Piles of substandard spices grew into hills,
        mountains, and, as many of you
        certainly learned, landfills
        everywhere filled with snow.
        We wondered what we should do.

Black cliffs of pepper, wide garlic salt peaks.
    Our boot soles stained deep red from cinnamon.
        We trailed thyme down the halls.
        As you no doubt observed, rules
        were broken daily—you disobeyed
        yourselves. It was that cold.

Though our Waste Dispersal Supervisor, Patty,
    tried very hard to work, she could not even name
        two girls in the wedding party
        photo collage atop her desk.
        (Those of you who fail to attend
        company picnics might understand.)

One noon, Patty went out to lunch with tall Phil.
    In his warm car, recalling the bridesmaids dresses—
        peach silk—and, finally, their names,
        she heard the radio warn: Stay home,
        avoid all icy highways, the city's
        sand and salt supplies are depleted!

The answer was simple, like holding Phil in the parking lot.
    Patty called Public Works. This was the beginning of things.
        All that night, trucks hauled away
        our garlic salt. That night, parsley
        dusted moonlight fell down green,
        melting dark sidewalks and streets.

(Some of you may gossip, watching when they exit
    the complex together, but their touching is not about sex—
        it is due to muddy snow puddles
        in the lobby, soft cafeteria apples,
        4 o'clock calls from the coast.)
    By dawn the roads were safe again

and whole neighborhoods smelled of remembered meals.
    A trip to the frozen backyard shed became your kitchen,
        redolent with the first holiday
        dinner after a father's death.
        You ate in dreams, walked places,
        stopped in the driveways of lost friends.

This is to inform you that our mayor kissed Patty,
    gave her a brass key to the city, an inscribed plaque.
        She wanted to give Phil the key
        but knew she couldn't. Continents
        of paprika still require disposal.
        All suggestions shall be considered.

CARDIGAN

Sweater slung from both shoulders
    of the chair, moth-eaten, seed pearls small as baby teeth

scattered down the placket—what the mother
    wore, pacing ovals at the school bus stop, white cashmere

yoked at the neck, O hero's cape . . .
    All summer, despite an arctic office chill, her daughter

ignores it. When she swivels to retrieve
    a fax, the sleeves flare out, mime goodbye, then fall slack.

STORY CITY, IOWA

We wander the craft booths mumbling the song
of the disappointed newcomers—moody, inconsolable,
sick of locals insisting we could love anyplace, if only
we would try. *Velkommen* to the annual Summer Festival
of Scandinavian Heritage, weekend of funnel cakes, kringle,
clog dance lessons on the green. Viking floats, lefse,
salted cod on this corner, lingonberry jam on the next.

> But two thousand miles west,
> months before the move,
> this town was our salvation,
> twenty miles north of new jobs.

> Imagine, we told friends,
> a place actually called Story City!
> And so, we packed crates,
> consoling ourselves with its creation.

We named the main street Denouement Avenue, bordered
by little stores with strange, meticulous window displays
(the shopkeepers' way to teach the weight of detail). Conflict?
Tornadoes and foreclosures. No wonder the tellers get migraines,
cash bad checks—everyone's surname is Protagonist.
And nights at home, their families are melancholy or ecstatic,
the result of childhoods spent on the cusp of epiphany.

> This morning, when the Union Pacific
> train whistles woke us,
> loud boys were already blazing
> side streets in rusted-out sedans,

> tossing crushed beer cans at trees.
> Restless, quarreling, we cursed them,
> grabbed maps, finally driving
> here to find our Story City.

Now lightning like rickrack trims the town's hem, yet we still
can't guzzle phosphates or clog dance. Even the instructor's
red skirt becomes our discontent, embroidered, inert in the heat,
though beautiful. Learn to love anyplace? If true, all entrances
must be marked *Beginning,* all exits *The End.* Then watch
this town self-destruct—because to every woman on the street
every man is the momentary, singular object of her desire.

SUNDAY AFTERNOON PALINDROME

They buy frozen orange juice, bread, eggs, then leave
Counting their change. Small brown sack balanced
Against her hip, she lags yards behind his shadow.
Keys and coins peal deep in his trenchcoat pockets,
Khaki cloth resurrected on this day of ransacked trees.
He lopes to the car, coattails snapping and talking back
At the wind—almost aloft, the lift of canvas wings . . .
Storm mornings, her students giddy from forecasts of snow,
She would show their favorite movies, *Pioneers of Flight,*
Path to Kitty Hawk: Animated bird-men leaping off blind
Cliffs and campaniles, courageous monks left blind,
Maimed, because their feathered limbs failed to echo flight.
How the children cheered as the credits rolled into snow,
Anticipating the projector's gift of reversal, splintered wings
Instantly whole could soar the crumpled adventurers back
To departure, their apparatus upswept from ravines and trees . . .
Last night the clocks turned back, cramming winter's pockets
Full with light. This is her dreaded season, long shadows
In the den by noon tipping the house off balance,
Her garden dim and inverted, gutters clotting with leaves.

TITANIC CLEARANCE

i.   *Buona Mattina*

Landlocked, midwestern,
all summer the Kroger manager practices rolling his R's,
    hawking the pyramids of videos

    as though the romantic star
were not DiCaprio but Leonardo himself,
    bewildered in seaweed

    at the endcap of Lane 3,
brushes, notebooks & easel salvaged
    from the scalloped cardboard sea . . .

ii.   *Key Fob*

Adrift in a cylinder of glycerin,
hull unscathed, the two-inch liner glides outbound,
    captained by the day's transactions:

    Rummage in your pocket
for spare change till the ship lists violently starboard—
    deck chairs splinter as the stern

    jackknifes across the sky . . .
Steerage immigrants leap from portholes, weeping,
    new lives heavy in their valises.

iii.   *Advance to Gangway*

The north Atlantic's waves break
in the den, though in the board game, no souls
    need be lost—spun well,

the blue diamond heart
catapults third-class passengers from Steerage
    up to Promenade. To win,

board a lifeboat, elbowing
out the robber baron's bejeweled wife, whose rubies
    plummet, useless, to the surf.

iv.   *Inventory*

In September, loudspeaker
grazias perfected, the manager dismantles the displays.
    The little memorabilia that remains—

a few sweatshirts, mugs, games—
he'll work into his weekly subliminal Specials:
    "Frosty iceberg lettuce

Fresh frozen fillets!"
intoned from his crow's nest above the store's
    cool expanse of lanes.

ADVECTION

And on Mondays and Wednesdays we intone
in adjacent classrooms, divided by slipshod
sheetrock and a white expanse of dry-erase—

thus the local affiliate weatherman finds
his pauses filled with half-assed freewrite prompts
while I disclose *vorticity* in a muted Indiana drawl.
Yes, he is as puny as you believed,
and his pilling, broadcast-grey suit drifts
across bones when he crosses the quad. In the stairwell,
his rabbit face reads mine: My love, *he knows*.

Bemused, unembarrassed, he locks my gaze, refusing
to look away. He knows that, unprepared,
I've cribbed his lesson plans and extracted you.

THE GREEK WEEK TORNADO

Ames, Iowa

Wrested from sleep, the students, hungover,
    rush onto their balconies
    pulling up boxer shorts
        or embarrassed
in bright silk teddies

    to watch the violet-black anvil cloud
        navigate northeast,
        mistaken zeppelin
          moving
    toward the dorms, stadium,

        maybe the downtown . . . payback time
        for a warm spring Saturday—
        nachos, sex, and vodka punch?
        Despite
        their excesses, the yard's mulch

    of debris offers absolution. No sirens,
        no crouching in cellars—
        Two weeks before finals,
        all warning
    systems fail. The red-haired

girl in 3-F swings a boom box and turns
    the evangelists from Boone
    up loud; their weathercasts
        are whispered
from an almighty source: whose corncrib,

whose elevator, cited simultaneously
as the storm destroys them.
Her family isn't mentioned
but she sees
their shelter belt of elms from here . . .

Under the announcer a Wurlitzer plays slowly
as sunrise turns her nightgown
transparent. She is beautiful,
the boys in 3-E
realize, her collarbone a perfect crossbow.

THREE

*The house we were born in is more than an embodiment
of home, it is also an embodiment of dreams.*

—Gaston Bachelard, *The Poetics of Space*

MAMMATOCUMULUS

O narrow luncheonette on Broad Street,
plastic éclairs bleached violet by the storefront
window sun—half-sleeping, daughter riveted
to my breast, again I revisit The Bow Knot,
twenty-six years after my grandmother called
a cab on a sloppy February noon & ventured out
to eat her last lunch. Egg salad on rye toast, a few
pickle chips, some tea. She watched the lazy susan
whirl a plate of cardboard petit fours & thought
of her stillborn son, my father's shadow brother
who spoke in his dreams. Then she walked home
against a raw wind off the Navesink; the clouds
stuffed with seagulls, circling down, down, beaks
pointed toward the tassel on her green plaid tam.

FOR SALE BY OWNER

Here is the house that no one will buy:
Cape Cod saltbox slapped up at the prairie's edge,
moored to a subdivision of faux fieldstone chateaus

and red roof haciendas, the last lot before backyard sod

splices back to farmland. Five bedrooms, three baths,
oak trim, beveled glass, nearly new yet abandoned
by every realtor in town. Even the hard-sell

redhead was stymied—triple garage spotless,

her secret tips for domestic adornment well done.
Daylight basement, master suite . . . but on taut
October weekends many drove up I-35 only to return

to Des Moines disquieted. Sundeck, mini-solarium,

lopsided garbage bag jack o'lanterns, plastic skeletons
flailing in the new sumacs. Attic dormers, marble foyer . . .
and in February this house featured three small sons

sculpting snow presidents to flank the driveway;

huge Washington and Lincoln, proficient depictions,
until a thaw melted the monuments into Easter Island
men in tricornes and toppers whose tunnel eyes

glared down the cul-de-sac for weeks.

Spacious pantry, breakfast nook . . . but last May
this was the house playing bad Bach, the daughter
repeating painstaking bars of *Joy of Man's Desiring,*

determined to master embouchure, hit high E's on key.

Prospective buyers pulled up, heard the flute, fled—
Summer! Owner must sacrifice! Where are the buyers
tonight? The mother scatters beach glass in her flower beds;

inside, her youngest son is silhouetted against cornfields

touching their backyard. Shirtless, his torso arced
back in smooth contour, he holds an orangeade jug
high above his mouth and deeply drinks.

Driving home, just then, the realtor realizes

she is passing the house no one would buy. It was the view,
she decides, that extinct grain elevator a few acres east,
bleached parallelograms empty in the evening sun,

an inscrutable volume problem in a child's math book.

FROZEN KENTUCKY SHRINE

Blued in his cobalt sweats,
58 Derby Place surveys his backyard:

Wind chime, windmill, and his brass *To Dad*
Inscribed pinwheel—faceted beneath fresh
Rinds of ice. Last week the crocuses rose
Around the dog pens, three months early,
While the lawn greened and grew. Go raise
Your Wildcat flag, said the wife, so he did,
Flummoxed by bumblebees grazing his ankles,
By the suncatcher caught with inapt light.

A game ago, the point guard's wrist snapped.
A game ago, they lost. Downstairs, the mascot
Of the house dozes open-mouthed, scowling
At some secret of her afternoon's sleep.
Her drool, intimate, repulsive, dampens
The upholstery. He can't remember
Ever missing her scent or that timbre
Of her terse *hello*. Look at the crocus

Blooms—violet pits beset by brittle fruit.
But the dogs shouldn't shed in December.

Turbulence, the Truck Driver, and the Waitress

Splash of ginger ale on my jeans, a fierce
jolt beneath the jet's belly—grinning, the attendants
scutter to their jumpseats and buckle up. Just weather,

our captain assures, then to calm us with diversion,
    switches on the Wide World of Sports Skating Report.
        Puccini, distant and tinny, bleats through my headset,

        the video monitors fill: Spread-eagled, revolving,
    body aloft on her partner's palm, our heroine mimics
glee for the cameras. *Pendulum lift in star position,*

the broadcaster murmurs, wedging his commentary
    between soprano, cello and violins, the aria splintered
        by his parentheticals—*Side by side double Salchows,*

        oh her shoulder rotation was off. But the entire arena
rises for the thirty-year-old underdogs with day jobs,
whoops at each imperfect camel sit spin and axel jump,

loving even the couple's simple cakewalks across the rink,
    obstinate, continuous cameos etched into ice,
        which the judges deem skewed—his back recurvate,

        her blades pointing Northwest instead of due North.
The plane lurches, veers left. *Finale triple toe loops.*
The pair wins the Bronze. Now comes ABC's Vaseline-lensed

montage of their real lives: Our hero dwarfed by his big rig
    posing at a desert rest stop, cacti, the sunset glow
        a tocsin on the interstate horizon behind him.

Cut to tight shots of hawks, the vast parking lot,
   tourists licking vanilla cones in the heat. Inside,
our heroine delivers dupes to the cooks, then hurries back,

glossy with sweat, to circle the crowded counters,
   her silver tray packed with burger platters, perched
      on one strong arm, held just above the heads of the diners.

EDWARD HOPPER WATCHING *THE PETRIFIED FOREST,* 1936

When I don't feel in the mood for painting
I go to the movies for a week or more.
I go on a regular movie binge!
　　　　　　—Hopper to Richard Lahey Papers

BAR-B-Q　　　BAR-B-Q　　　BAR-B-Q

the only creed the mesa may ever know . . .
giant fossil trees dreaming eons of sweet smoked meat,
biscuits, petrol, chocolates, cigars,

and orders of creamed corn soup,
the Daily Special centered in a deep porcelain bowl,
yellow just whiter than autumn sun

on apartment walls. But this diner,
crammed with Duke Mantee and his desperado gang,
drunk Gramps Maple and Boze,

the fattish halfback turned pumpboy,
is too cluttered—a claustrophobia of confessions,
gunshots, and fervid broadcasters

warning travelers against desert routes,
though they'll miss the view at dusk, pomegranates
splattered in the painted hills, lingering

until a train passes, and a passenger
looks up from her book because the compartment
flushed like a sudden, ripening fruit.

Bananas and waxy apples, toothpicks,
matches—rearranged and dusted by the bored waitress
who reads Villon beneath the pumps

and imagines Paris, her job in a café
beside the quais, leaving the late kitchen to return
        to a building, dim stairway and banister,

        steps collapsing into an accordion,
then her room, one window watching the courtyard,
        bottle of wine and half a loaf of bread.

    True, that's a continent and an ocean away—
she's still a hostage in Arizona, and a philosophical hobo
        has ordered a burger, ennui, and her heart.

    Let's swig a shot of rye while we wait:
Duke's dame double-crossed him and the squad cars'
        tiny sirens draw close in the dark.

    At the long counter, the gang loads rifles
full with extra rounds. This joint is too easy to case
        at night—lit sprawl of triangles, cubes,

        and tumbleweed perched at the edge
of flatlands—maps, beer, Coca-Cola, and neon pulsing
        the only creed the mesa may ever know . . .

    BAR-B-Q   BAR-B-Q   BAR-B-Q

1813

—after Thomas Love Peacock's
Memoirs of Percy Bysshe Shelley

Miles still to Bracknell, as the woman shifted
Three parcels across her mountainous lap,
And in that instant, accordion of skirts lifted,

Petticoats above the knees, Shelley watched
Her calves collapse, molten flesh like poultices
Leaking through sackcloth, tubers gone to rot,

The carriage air fetid and contagious.
He swaddled his head with scarves—a filter
Created too late; abruptly weak, flushed,

Her affliction routed through his veins.
Who insisted that travel was a tonic?
Arriving at the inn, his intricate skein

Of symptoms unwound and unwound—an itch
Beneath his chin, nematodes burrowing deep
Within the lymph glands, an aching right wrist

Sure prelude to that arm's unbridled girth.
He dreamt of dead elephants floating
In lakes, then woke feverish, the nightshirt's

Wrinkles stamped onto his chest. Mirror-bound,
He monitored each ruddy crease until it faded,
His neck became porcelain again, and a barren

Day seemed utterly impossible. How to recapture
Those dusks with Ianthe, pacing, his daughter
Close at his breast, no fear of lesions or fissures,

Singing *Yáhmani* into her vanilla hair,
Yáhmani, Yáhmani, Yáhmani, Yáhmani,
A road, horses cantering through summer air,

His three syllables of secret journey
Chanted to invoke a child's solid sleep,
And dreams of the distances between cities.

And if the ulcers erupted, seeping purple,
Who would whisper, and lull her, and sing?
Certain nights even the trees were instigators,

And the wind. Branch shadows, dark hairs
Stirring on knuckles, blotches on his hands—
Weather and illusion would turn to portent

As the poet, comparing his wrinkles and limbs
With companions, contorted the evening party
To prods and pinches. *Show your thumb!*

How thick is your ankle? Are we the same?
Flex your elbow! His guests always obliged
Though this warm evidence never calmed him;

Their perfect correspondences, foot against foot,
Thigh to thigh, were not enough. Only Peacock
Could quell his friend's panic, retrieving books,

Quoting Lucretius through open parlor windows:
Est elephas morbus, qui propter flumina Nili,
Listen, only in Egypt, *Gignitur Aegypto* . . .

That woman in the carriage was fat, nothing more.
A balm of rationales spoken aloud each night,
Until one dawn his body returned, proportioned,

Flesh taut and pores invisible. The sweet skin
Beside Ianthe's left earlobe, *Yáhmani,* her scent
Was what he'd missed the most, the whole inn

Still asleep and her cradle brimming with sun.
Outside the landscape was hedgerows and rills.
No pyramids or sphinxes squatted on the horizon.

Fruit & Garden Mart

Plum-nosed, slippers brimmed with veins,
she bumper cars her cart into mine, badgering,
four times, too close, *Is this Beethoven?*
Listen (that familiar fermented breath)
to the cashier's radio, tell her no, it's Clapton.

You're always wrong, she yells, extracting a bust
from her heap of egg rock, mums, and phlox—
Is THIS Beethoven? She thrusts the plastic face
at my face: Demeter, marbleized, a crappy relic

destined to rest in mulch. Informed it's a goddess,
she mutters *I've forgotten what they all look like*
then abandons the head on a mound of potatoes.
And so the morning's decapitation is done,
all the bored eyes upon her, ringed with Idaho earth.

OPHTHALMOLOGICAL

Now showing on the waiting room Telemonitor—
   father's left eyeball, lids curled back, clamped,
      while his compatriots (parents and spouses

tranquilized, in queue) study the incision
   without flinching. This procedure's star:
      his cataract, seventy years of scenes obscured

by milky scrim, all past roles suctioned then cast
   down to an imbroglio of cells in a biohaz bucket.
      Minutes later, you're directed to Recovery

where again he calls you by your mother's name.
   Betadine-stained, his face becomes a headshot
      when you feed him Lorna Doones and tea.

The nurse, an ingénue blonde, brings more sweets.
   Semiconscious, he flirts, proffers boyhood
      stories as aphrodisiac—first girl, dead dog,

lost friends, and his standby, the Hindenburg
   above the Queens bungalow, borough shadowed
      by the airship's weekly trips. But O dirigible,

in this post-op hallucination, the gondola forgets
   to explode, berthing quietly on Rockaway Beach.
      Six-years-old, he's there playing hobo, bindle

crammed full of sand. The passengers disembark,
   hands chained, spanned to the surf, they beckon
      for your small father to bow with them.

Their audience, the sunset, applauds refracted gold.
 —Ointment, saline, the nurse tends his rheumy eye.
  Been to Lakehurst? she asks, then straightens

his huge starlet sunglasses. He's groggy, silent.
 How far is it? 20 miles? 25? I'll take a drive
 on my next day off. I bet it's something to see.

THE STORY OF THE DAY

The birds will open your house with their wings,
    Frail bones against the hinges, doorframes
Stunned, and as the eaves unweave, the roof leaves
    Just a parasol of air. We try to predict routes,
Conjuring wind charts and weather maps—
    How far could they fly from these October trees,
Or the countries in your closet, or the ceiling
    Moons and planets orbiting only within
Your cupped palms? In this room, dark corners
    Explained, the night light hovers on the wall
Like a cloud. You settle in my arms, your body
    Beginning a mime of my breathing. You wish
For sky, shingles scattering, as we listen for
    Feathers, insistent thrushes at the sill.

WORKING THE NARRAGANSETT NIGHT OWL

*. . . On the last Sunday in October, when most communities set
clocks back at 2 AM, Amtrak trains, will hold back
for one hour to be "on time"—not early—according to
local time at subsequent stations . . .*

         —Amtrak Northeast Timetable

Where the lost hour is lost matters most. Idle on a siding
outside Westerly yards, or shelved before the twin mouths

of the Charlestown tunnels, passengers will drowse in darkness,
wake to extinct locomotives bracketing the tracks and profiles

across the aisle—the half-faces suggestions of resemblances—
a bully from childhood, or worse, a lover long known dead.

But if we depart on schedule, our hold-back should be Mystic,
midway on the landbridge before the trestle's web; brackish air,

river so near the tracks that in fog the waiting train floats
above its anchor. My first year on the Owl, we'd only passed

Providence when my pocketwatch turned to 2:00. We braked
to sit at the city's edge, on tracks between tall warehouses,

bakeries, and garages abandoned soon after being built.
Small fires stained the windows orange—squatters, I supposed,

living on the top stories, behind relics of advertisements
once painted on the bricks . . . *Be utifu   Co plex   n* . . .

pink-lidded jar of cold cream mother stowed by the sink
. . . *oke   Opti   o* . . . father's chewed, smoldering cigar . . .

At the front of my car, a man began to moan; a low wailing
as if mourning his wife and child. I shook him until he quieted

but from seats by the washroom came snide moans, a mockery.
Animals! someone shouted. Later, when we jerked forward,

at the same moment we'd arrived, the man's keening resumed.
This is why I worship exactitude: pulling out of Back Bay

the second the gantry lights signal green, anticipating arrivals
of stations solely by the realignment creak then lapse of noise

as the engineer slows to round a sharp curve. Now at 1:50
a charred, damp odor enters the coaches—disperses—

the Westerly woolen mills gone, precisely on schedule—
we'll make the Mystic hold-back. Two quick track switches,

the reading lights flicker twice, then a rare trade—the ring
of slow brake on smooth rails slurs to sail tack clanging

on masts. All the crew steps down. We stand in the ballast,
kicking stones, the locomotive a low drone high above us,

the sky scrimshawed with clippers and whalers, thatched roofs,
steeples, stars. Flasks and cigarettes appear but we don't talk.

We remember *bulwark, hawser, jib*—words we only truly learned
as children but retrieve waiting on the outskirts of a tourist seaport,

where from this distance, restorations are irrelevant. Greater
mates to each other than those who wait at home, all year

we rest upright in our seats, doze before the New Haven rush,
wake to a slightly rank, uniformed shoulder which we tap awake.

Once each October, none of this happens, no passengers dream—
we celebrate the anniversary of companioned nothingness.

PENSIONE CRISTALLO

Every day a beautiful sentence
You must memorize before bed.
For mystery I will hide them.
Search between the jams at breakfast,
Beneath your plate of morning bread,
This is how you will learn my language:
Sono stata in montagna per due settimane
é tutto quello che ho visto, mi é piacuto.

Music tonight, our summer festival,
But just now it is so quiet,
Mi é piacuto, mi é piacuto, repeat this
And tell where you've traveled.
Keep me company with the television.
Rock Hudson was quite a handsome man,
I enjoy so much watching this movie
Because I had a lover who resembled him,
Especially his eyes, how we collect
And collect pieces of people,
I have been with no one since he left.

Mornings in this city I see women
Lower baskets from their windows
And pull up the world with ropes.
This is what we were for each other,
The daily paper, coffee, pears,
We were the puller and basket filler,
Tomatoes, basil, wine.
And best was to close the shutters
And take naps in the late afternoons,
Just before the weather turned to winter,
Oh my friend, upstairs in our room,
Those were the nicest hours.

Must I curse the baker's shoulders,
A stranger's wrists, this violet light?
Tutto quello che ho visto, mi é piacuto
Everything I saw, I liked.

Notes

"JoAnne from Travel Accounting." In memory of Lora Iovine Ilari.

"Memorandum re: Garlic Salt." The incident in the poem is based on events described by Perry Beeman in *The Des Moines Register*, January 19 and 23, 1993.

"At Bracknell" and "1813." Both poems are informed by Thomas Love Peacock's *Memoirs of Percy Bysshe Shelley* and by *A View of the Nervous Temperament*, an 1807 medical text by Thomas Trotter, MD. Trotter's book was revered by Shelley and his contemporaries.

Acknowledgements

The author would like to thank her friends, family, and colleagues for their advice and support. Extra thanks to Catherine Sasanov, Mary Swander, Alan Williamson, Joan Wojan, Mike McWilliams, Rebecca Morgan Frank, Adam Day, and Bernice Jailer.

Thank you to the Stanford University Department of English for a Wallace Stegner Creative Writing Fellowship, The Iowa State University Department of English, The Kentucky Arts Council, and The North Carolina Arts Council.

About the Author

Martha Greenwald is from Middletown, New Jersey. Her poems have appeared in several journals including *Best New Poets 2008, Slate, The Threepenny Review, Poetry, The Sycamore Review* and *Shenandoah*. A former Wallace Stegner Fellow, she has received awards from the arts councils of North Carolina and Kentucky.